Emotional Intelligence Guide

How to Implement Emotional Intelligence at Your Work & Get Rid of Negative Thoughts

Zach Roger

Copyright © 2018 Zach Roger

All rights reserved.

© COPYRIGHT 2019 BY **ZACH ROGER** – ALL RIGHTS RESERVED.

This book is geared towards providing exact and reliable information in regards to the topic and issue covered. The publication is sold with the idea that the publisher is not required to render an accounting, officially permitted, or otherwise, qualified services. If advice is necessary, legal or professional, a practiced individual in the profession should be ordered.

- From a Declaration of Principles which was accepted and approved equally by a Committee of the American Bar Association and a Committee of Publishers and Associations.

In no way is it legal to reproduce, duplicate, or transmit any part of this book in either electronic means or in printed format. Recording of this publication is strictly prohibited and any storage of this book is not allowed unless with written permission from the publisher. All rights reserved.

The information provided herein is stated to be truthful and consistent, in that any liability, in terms of inattention or otherwise, by any usage or abuse of any policies, processes, or directions contained within is the solitary and utter responsibility of the recipient reader. Under no circumstances will any legal responsibility or blame be held against the publisher for any reparation, damages, or monetary loss due to the information herein, either directly or indirectly.

Respective authors own all copyrights not held by the publisher.

The information herein is offered for informational purposes solely and is universal as so. The presentation of the information is without a contract or any type of guarantee assurance.

The trademarks that are used are without any consent, and the publication of the trademark is without permission or backing by the trademark owner. All trademarks and brands within this book are for clarifying purposes only and are the owned by the owners themselves, not affiliated with this document.

CONTENTS

Emotional intelligence 2.0: How to Practically Implement Intelligence at Your Work

	Introduction	1
1	Develop Emotional Self-Awareness	2
2	Become Emotionally Aware of Others	5
3	Control the Emotional Environment	8
4	Inspire Motivation	11
5	Master Social Skills	14
6	Establish Accountability	17
7	Improve Overall Health and Wellbeing	20
	Conclusion	23

Emotional intelligence 2.0: How to Get Rid of Negative Thoughts

	Introduction	27
1	Your Personal Litany of Ills	29
2	Confronting Your Malicious Subconscious	32
3	How I Did it	37
4	Alert and Attentive	42
	Conclusion	47

Emotional Intelligence 2.0

How to Practically Implement Emotional Intelligence at Your Work

Zach Roger

ZACH ROGER

INTRODUCTION

Emotional intelligence is something that is absolutely vital for anyone who wants to achieve any level of success in life. This is especially true in the workplace environment. It is a fact that every job causes stress and anxiety in a person's life. If left unchecked, that stress and anxiety can begin to affect the way a you think, the words you say and the actions you perform.

This is where emotional intelligence comes into play. By developing emotional intelligence, you can reduce stress and anxiety, thereby eliminating the influence they have on your life. Furthermore, by improving your emotional health and wellbeing, you can achieve greater success in all areas of your life, including such things as relationships, personal goals and even your career. This book will reveal several techniques that will enable you to develop emotional intelligence at your work, thus enabling you to take control of your emotions, and subsequently your life overall.

1 DEVELOP EMOTIONAL SELF-AWARENESS

The workplace is one of the most emotionally charged environments that you will encounter in your life. Full of stress, anxiety, competitive drive and even desperation, it can create all sorts of negative emotional responses within your mind, thus influencing not only how you think but also what you say and even how you act. Unfortunately, most people allow their workplace to control their emotional state, resulting in a number of regrettable actions that can cause significant problems for a person, up to and including the loss of their job. The key to overcoming this problem is to increase your emotional intelligence.

Emotional intelligence is the process of being aware of emotions, how they influence you and the events that trigger specific emotional responses. While this process has several aspects, including being aware of the emotions of others, the single aspect that is more important than any other is becoming aware of your own emotions. This is the condition where you are constantly in touch with how you feel at any time and in any circumstance. By being aware of your feelings you will be able to prevent them from taking control of your thoughts, words and actions. This will ensure that you maintain total control of your life no matter how emotionally charged your work environment is. Therefore, the first thing you need to do is to develop emotional self-awareness.

Be aware of your feelings at all times

Emotional self-awareness begins when you take the time to recognize exactly how you feel on a regular basis. Too often people get caught up in the hustle and bustle of the day, causing them to ignore their thoughts and feelings, and because they never take the time to assess how they feel, they allow all sorts of negative emotions to grow in their heart and mind, resulting in high levels of stress and anxiety that can take control of their lives.

This is often experienced when a person gets home from a long day at work, in which their stress levels were increased all throughout the day. By the time they walk through the door of their house they are so stressed that it takes only the smallest of things to set them off in a rage. How many times have you allowed your anger and stress to influence how you interact with your spouse or loved ones? For many people, this has happened many times than they can even remember. This is because anyone who is not emotionally self-aware is vulnerable to this situation.

Fortunately, emotional self-awareness can help you avoid taking out negative thoughts and feelings on those you love. The first step is to develop the habit of taking random moments to step back and ask yourself exactly how you feel. Most of the time you will have an immediate answer, as you are probably stressed or tired when at work. Alternatively, you may find that you are happy and relaxed, especially if you like your job and the people you work with. Whether your emotions are positive or negative, it is equally important to always be aware of them.

Once you have determined your emotional state you can take a moment to analyze that state and whether or not you should take any actions to correct it. In the event that you are highly stressed you might want to take a break and get some fresh air. Simply walking away from whatever you are doing can be enough to reduce the negativity in your mind. You may go a step further and get a coffee drink to help restore your mood. Sometimes something as simple as a coffee drink, a donut or some other indulgence can trigger positive emotions that will help calm any stress or anxiety you are feeling. Doing this on a regular basis will prevent your stress levels from getting out of hand, and this will ensure that you have better control over your words and actions, thereby keeping you from lashing out at friends and loved ones at the end of a long and stressful day.

Exercise self-control

Being aware of your emotions is only half of the process of becoming emotionally self-aware. The other half of the process is exercising self-control. This is where so many people struggle the most. Even if you are aware of your feelings, if you don't exercise self-control you can still take out your emotions on those you love. Needless to say, this only results in creating even more stress and anxiety, and not to mention guilt and regret.

The key, therefore, is to develop the discipline of emotional self-control.

One of the most common methods for practicing self-control is to count to ten before speaking or acting when you know that you are stressed or angry. This is particularly helpful when you are in the midst of a situation that is emotionally charged, such as an argument or any other similarly unsettling event at work. The reason counting to ten is effective is that it prevents you from reacting mindlessly to something someone else says or does. By taking a few extra seconds before responding you can switch the gears of your mind, thereby changing your response from an emotional one to an intellectual one. In other words, taking a few seconds will ensure that you always think before you act.

Self-control is much more than your responses to a situation. It also affects your ability to protect yourself from negatively charged events and people, thereby reducing the effect they have on your emotional state. As mentioned before, if you know you are stressed you should take a moment to do something for yourself such as get some coffee, a donut or something else that will lift your spirits. This is taking control of where you are in order to regain control over your emotions.

Another example is to avoid from going somewhere or doing something stressful if you know that you are already feeling high levels of anxiety in your heart and mind. By not engaging in an argument, or not taking on a project that will further deteriorate your mental wellbeing you can ensure that your stress levels never get out of control. Thus, self-control isn't just about taking charge of how your emotional state affects you, but it is also about taking control of the things that influence your emotional state. The more control you have over these areas, the more control you will have over every aspect of your life.

2 BECOME EMOTIONALLY AWARE OF OTHERS

Once you have become emotionally self-aware the next step is to become emotionally aware of others. This is the process of recognizing and understanding the emotional state of those around you, specifically those you are interacting with, especially at work. Just as a lack of emotional self-awareness can cause you to speak and act in ways that are harmful to others, lacking emotional awareness of others will also have the same effect. If you don't realize that the person you are speaking to is stressed or distraught you can say or do something inadvertently that can make their situation even worse. Needless to say, this is how small things get blown out of proportion all of the time.

Alternatively, the more aware you are of another person's emotions, the better your chances of connecting to that person by saying or doing the right thing. This will help to prevent stressful situations from getting out of hand, which is a very valuable skill to have in any workplace. By recognizing that the person you are speaking to is stressed or angry you can better choose your words in order to calm their emotional state. Not only will this prevent matters from getting out of hand, but it will also improve the results of any conversations you have. Instructions will be followed more effectively, and feelings won't be hurt by unnecessary bluntness or any seeming lack of concern. This is a sure way to maintain high levels of morale in the workplace even in the midst of highly stressful situations.

Carefully observe verbal communication

Becoming emotionally aware of others is a simple matter of taking the time to carefully observe verbal communications. When you are talking to your colleagues at work, take the time to analyze how they are talking to you. If they are saying very little, and speaking in a low tone, then the chances that they are feeling overwhelmed or vulnerable are high. Thus, if you add to their workload, or criticize them on their performance you might push them to the breaking point. In this situation you should take extra care to ensure that they feel supported and valued.

On the other hand, if they speak in an aggressive manner, with a raised voice and an abrupt tone they are probably very angry. Needless to say, anything you say to a person in this frame of mind will either be taken the wrong way or it will simply go in one ear and out the other. In such a situation it is critical to take the time to ask them what is causing them to feel so angry. Only when you bring them down from their anger, demonstrating that you are there to help, will you be able to communicate with them effectively. The important thing is to prevent the situation from becoming any worse than it already is.

Ideally, when you are speaking to another person you want to see positive indicators in their verbal communication with you. A calm tone of voice, for example, will indicate that they are calm and confidant, which is a good thing in any environment. Furthermore, if they engage in a conversation, providing feedback, asking questions or simply restating your words to show that they are on the same page, this indicates that they are very happy and comfortable with both the situation and their standing with you. Ideally, this is the type of verbal communication you want to encourage and promote with everyone at all times.

In addition to analyzing the verbal communication between you and another person it is also useful to observe the verbal communication that takes place between other employees. Too little conversation can indicate distrust, or that some employees simply don't like each other. It can also indicate shyness or low self-esteem, things that can be addressed by engaging in team building activities. Abrupt and agitated tones can indicate hostility or overly competitive tendencies. Again, these issues can be addressed through team building exercises as well as through one-on-one counseling.

Ironically enough, one of the best forms of verbal communication between employees is laughter. While most people see laughter as a sign that things aren't being taken seriously enough, a healthy amount of laughter can actually indicate confidence, a strong sense of community and, most importantly, a strong sense of optimism. Therefore, if you hear employees laughing and having a good time, rather than suspecting that they aren't getting any work done, recognize that they are probably getting their best work done. Smiling, laughing employees are the least stressed, most trustworthy and more often than not, the most productive you will ever find.

Carefully observe non-verbal communication

Another way in which you can become emotionally aware of others is by carefully observing non-verbal communication. This is the art of being able to read a person's body language. By observing how a person stands, sits, walks and physically interacts with others you can tell a great deal about their emotional health and wellbeing. There are times when certain elements can mean more than one thing, however, when you put things into proper context you can always get a clear picture of how a person is feeling by the way they appear physically.

Eye contact is perhaps the most important element of non-verbal communication. If the person you are talking to constantly looks at the floor they are either expressing low self-esteem or even guilt of some kind. This can be a good thing to recognize depending on the conversation you are having. If you suspect a person is guilty of wrongdoing and they fail to make eye contact when you address them your suspicions are probably true. If a person looks beyond you and to the side when you talk to them they are either bored or disinterested in what you are saying. Needless to say, that is never a good sign. Ideally, a person should make regular and comfortable eye contact with you. This indicates that they are confident, engaging and interested in what you have to say.

A person's arms can tell a great deal about their state of mind as well. If the person you are talking to has their arms folded this usually suggests defensive feelings. Needless to say, this can indicate high levels of stress and low levels of self-esteem. This is especially true if their shoulders droop as well. Alternatively, if the person has their arms in a relaxed position, hanging straight down or resting on something this suggests that they are open to what you are saying. This is when conversations will produce the best results as the other person will be more receptive to anything and everything you have to say. Reading these simple signs can help you to choose the right words to ensure that you make the necessary connection to the person you are trying to communicate with.

3 CONTROL THE EMOTIONAL ENVIRONMENT

As mentioned earlier, a person's workplace is probably the most emotionally charged environment they will experience on a regular basis. While developing emotional awareness—both of yourself and those around you, is critical, it may not always be enough. This is particularly true in workplaces where the job is especially stressful. The simple truth is that emotions are influenced by external factors, just as much as words and actions are influenced by emotions. Thus, if the emotional environment of the workplace is left unchecked it can create levels of stress and anxiety that awareness alone won't be able to overcome.

Therefore, in order to have a better control over the emotional state of yourself and others while at work you need to learn to control the emotional environment itself. This can be done in several different ways, from maintaining positive dialogue with everyone to establishing systems and habits that reduce stress levels when followed. In the end, the more the effort you exert to create a positive environment, the more positive everyone will become. This can help to transform even the most challenging workplace into a place of happiness, contentment and satisfaction.

Reducing stress and fear of failure

One of the main causes of negativity in any workplace is basically stress itself. Unfortunately, any number of things can cause stress, so it is actually impossible to eliminate it from any workplace environment. However, certain steps can be taken to ensure that stress is significantly reduced, thereby improving the overall environment considerably. A good way to reduce stress is to ensure that expectations are always reasonable. While it may seem positive for a person to take on more and more tasks at any given time, the truth is that people can easily become overwhelmed in this way. Therefore, it is critical that deadlines are never unreasonable, that tasks are never too large to be handled, and that goals are always achievable.

A very common cause of stress and anxiety at work is multitasking. Again, at a first glance multitasking might seem like a sign of ambition and ability, however, studies have shown that multitasking is actually counterproductive in the end. One reason for this is that when a person is faced with several tasks at once their concentration levels decrease, largely because they have their mind going in multiple directions at the same time. Furthermore, the more the projects a person has ongoing at any given time, the more deadlines they face, the more accountability they experience and the more people they usually have to answer. Consequently, this will increase stress levels exponentially while actually reducing productivity. Therefore, avoid and prevent multitasking whenever possible.

Another significant cause of stress at the workplace is the fear of failure. If a person has a goal, task or target to accomplish there is the chance that they may succeed and there is also the chance that they may fail. When success seems more and more unlikely, stress and anxiety will increase to overwhelming levels, creating a negatively charged work environment. The best way to prevent this is to eliminate the fear of failure whenever possible. One way to do this is to have an open-door policy. Any time a person is unsure that they can achieve their objective they should feel welcome to come to you and ask for help. Even if you don't help directly you can find a solution that will put the person back on track for success. Being a source of help rather than a source of judgment will go a long way in eliminating any fear of failure and the negative emotional environment it can create.

Creating a positive environment

Reducing stress and the fear of failure in the workplace is only one side of the coin when it comes to controlling the emotional environment. The other side of the coin is to create a positive environment, one that is optimistic, relaxed and generally happy. Unfortunately, in most workplaces the focus is placed strictly on results, meaning that the emotional environment becomes increasingly toxic over time. The real tragedy is that such toxicity only serves to undermine results, not improve them. However, when you take the time to create a positive environment you can reduce and even eliminate such toxicity, thereby improving results as well as the emotional wellbeing of your employees.

Nothing creates a positive interpersonal environment more than the establishment of trust. When coworkers trust each other, they tend to enjoy their job more, thereby producing better results. Additionally, when employees trust their bosses, they tend to be more productive and loyal, usually staying with the company far longer than employees who don't trust the people they work for. The best way to establish trust is to avoid any actions that diminish trust. For example, never, EVER, engage in gossip or rumor spreading. Any time you are willing to talk about other people you will be seen as being untrustworthy, especially if you appear friendly to the people you gossip about. However, by never speaking about other people, except in a good way, you will induce trust and confidence in those around you.

Another way to establish trust is to make sure you are reliable. If you make a promise, always keep that promise no matter how much effort it takes or how much you might come to regret it. When you fail to keep the promises you make, your word will become meaningless, thereby reducing the trust others place in you. However, when you follow through on each and every promise your word will become rock solid in the minds of those you work with. Such trust will create a bond that money cannot buy. The important thing is to make sure that you encourage the same trustworthy actions in those around you, thereby creating a healthy and strong emotional environment for everyone.

4 INSPIRE MOTIVATION

Another vital way that can help you control the emotional environment of the workplace is to inspire motivation. One of the main causes of stress and anxiety within the workplace is a lack of motivation. Whenever people feel overworked, underappreciated and generally disillusioned with their job they will begin to lose the motivation that encourages them to put in their best effort. The end result is not only a lack-luster performance but also a loss of interest in the task at hand. Even worse, the longer a person lacks motivation, the more stressed they become by having a job that doesn't make them happy. Therefore, inspiring motivation is the key to creating a positive emotional environment.

Additionally, you can actually spread emotional intelligence to those around you through motivation. When you show people how to handle the pressures and stresses of the workplace environment through your own actions you can help them to develop better habits and behaviors of their own. This will cause them to develop emotional intelligence without even realizing it. The important thing is that you always demonstrate emotional intelligence in the things you say and do, thereby setting the standard for others to follow.

Lead by example

There are countless books available on the different styles of leadership and the benefits each style possesses. One thing most books will tell you is the importance of leading by example. While this may sound like a revolutionary concept, the truth of the matter is that every person in charge leads by example whether they realize it or not. If a manager overreacts to every little setback that they face they will encourage each and every employee to do the same. This is because they create the idea that setbacks are devastating by reacting the way they do. Therefore, even though they don't mean to, these managers increase the stress and anxiety in their environment by reacting in an emotionally charged way.

This makes a lot of sense when you realize that people are no different than animals in nature when it comes to learning. Every animal learns by watching and mimicking the actions of their parents or other animals. This is how ducks learn to swim, sparrows learn to fly and lions learn to hunt. While people are taught new skills at school or with the aid of instruction manuals, the same observational process is still present. Thus, people will develop skills and behaviors based on what they see and experience more than in any other way. This is why leading by example is so vital for controlling the emotional environment of any place, not just work.

Once you realize how leading by example works you can begin to use it to your advantage, as well as the advantage of those around you. The first thing to do is to actively avoid negative behavior. It's not enough to never appear to engage in negativity, however. Instead, you actually have to actively avoid and condemn it. One example of this is with how you react to setbacks. Every time something doesn't go according to plan you need to demonstrate your emotional intelligence in how you respond to the situation. Rather than getting stressed out and lashing out, simply show your confidence in being able to solve the problem at hand. Furthermore, demonstrate the fact that you don't see setbacks as problems in the first place. This will prove that your confidence is more than just a façade hiding your true feelings.

Another way to lead by example is to set the standard regarding principles and ethics. You can't expect others to take punctuality seriously if you are always late or behind schedule. However, when you show up at work on time each and every day and have tasks completed by their deadline, you will encourage others to focus their efforts on always being on time. Additionally, showing integrity is absolutely vital for creating a positive emotional environment. By always being honest with others you will encourage others to be honest with you. This will significantly reduce the stress and anxiety that comes from dishonesty, underhanded actions and other similar elements that only undermine a person's emotional stability.

Reward hard work and success

Numerous studies have shown that another effective way to inspire motivation in a person is to reward hard work and success. All too often the focus in any workplace environment is the consequence of failure. Many companies believe that the best way to get a person to perform at their best is to keep the threat of being fired for failure always present in their minds. Such methods have been shown to not only cause untold stress and anxiety, but to also undermine a person's performance rather than improving it. In the end it seems that negative motivation only ever leads to negative results.

Alternatively, it has been discovered that when people are rewarded for hard work and success they tend to perform better on a more regular basis. This is a critical point to understand when it comes to influencing the emotional wellbeing of those around you, especially in the workplace. Every time you reward a person for good behavior you will encourage them to continue behaving in the same way. This holds true for any aspect of performance. By showing appreciation for a job well-done you will encourage a person to continue to perform at their best level. The simple reason for this is that pleasure always beats fear as a motivator. Therefore, always be generous in rewarding those who put in good performances and produce positive results.

Perhaps the most important aspect of rewarding hard work and success is that it fosters a sense of teamwork within any workplace environment. The main reason for this is that most employees are aware of the fact that managers tend to get bonuses when they achieve their quotas. Unfortunately, the average employee is usually left empty handed, even though it was their hard work and effort that accomplished the goal. Subsequently, when you share the spoils of success with those who created the success in the first place it serves to make them feel more a part of the process. The more valuable employees feel they are, the more valuable their contribution will become, leading to even greater success as a result.

5 MASTER SOCIAL SKILLS

Any time you are in an environment where you have to interact with other people there is nothing more important than having good social skills. After all, if you can't communicate clearly with others, or you remain detached and aloof from those around you, your chances of success will suffer dramatically. This is especially true in any job that requires a team-oriented approach to accomplish tasks. The more you have to rely on the assistance or efforts of others, the more you need to be able to interact with them in a real and meaningful way. If you can't communicate your ideas clearly and effectively you won't be able to turn those ideas into reality.

Alternatively, if you can't understand what others are trying to convey you won't be able to produce the results they are looking for. This means that communication needs to be a two-way street. Not only do you need to make your ideas understood, but you also need to be able to understand the ideas and goals of others. Only when everyone involved can understand each other and the tasks at hand can a team have any chance of being successful. Therefore, if you want to increase your emotional intelligence it is critical that you master social skills.

Improve communication with others

Mastering social skills begins with the basic element of communication. No amount of positive interaction with people will be significant if it causes confusion or uncertainty. Again, one of the most important aspects of emotional intelligence is to reduce those factors that create negative emotions in the first place. Things like confusion, misunderstanding and doubt only serve to create the stress and anxiety that makes emotional intelligence harder to master. Therefore, it is vital that you improve your communication with others.

The first step in this process is to take the time to speak in a clear manner. All too often people rush through communications in an attempt to save time. Unfortunately, this usually leads to mistakes being made as a result of people being unsure of what they are supposed to do. Thus, rather than saving time, rushed communications, whether spoken or written, can actually cause problems and delays that take more time to fix. However, if you take the time to get your ideas across clearly you can save time by avoiding misunderstandings and the mistakes they can create.

Even if you speak in a clear and concise manner, others may not actually follow what you are trying to say. Therefore, it is also vital that you take the time to ask people you speak to whether or not they fully understand what you are saying. Getting their feedback in the moment will go a long way towards eliminating the confusion and uncertainty that can cause unnecessary stress and anxiety. Furthermore, by soliciting feedback you will increase the other person's sense of self-worth. The more you value their opinion, the more they will feel valued overall.

Another critical element for improved communication is the balance between passion and knowledge. Every time you talk to someone make sure you show positive emotional energy regarding the matter at hand. You won't get the other person interested in what you are saying if you aren't interested in it yourself. Additionally, make sure you are well informed regarding the matter at hand. If you seem unsure about your position, or how to accomplish the task at hand, you will only create doubt and frustration in the minds of others. Thus, good communication isn't just about speaking clearly, it's also about speaking passionately and with conviction.

Develop a strong sense of empathy

The most effective people in terms of social skills are those who possess a strong sense of empathy. This is also true as regards to emotional intelligence. One of the most effective ways of being emotionally intelligent is to understand your emotional perspective as well as the emotional perspective of those around you. In a way, this is the ability to enter another person's mind and see things through their eyes. The more you practice empathy, the more effective you will become at any type of interaction with other people.

This skill is critical whether you are a boss or a regular employee.

Sometimes a boss might come across as overly critical of your performance, raising their voice, appearing agitated and showing general frustration with you. If you take their behavior at face value you will only become anxious and defensive as a result. However, if you take a moment to consider things from their perspective you will realize just how desperate they actually are. More often than not your bosses have to answer bosses of their own, meaning that they have to answer for each and every setback encountered along the way. Subsequently, they are wholly dependent on your performance in order to achieve their goals. If your efforts aren't quite right, they will have to pay the price.

Once you realize that their aggression is actually a sign of desperation you can better understand their behavior. Subsequently, rather than becoming defensive or hurt you can seek to assure them that any mistakes will be corrected in a timely manner. Additionally, you can reassure them that you are wholly committed to the task in hand and that you desire success as much as they do. By responding this way, you will demonstrate that you are on their side, and that you are a part of the solution rather than a part of the problem. This will go a long way to calming their mood, which will improve your interaction with them exponentially.

6 ESTABLISH ACCOUNTABILITY

The whole concept of emotional intelligence can be summed up in a single word—control. People who lack emotional intelligence are those who lack control over their emotional wellbeing, and thus their thoughts, words and even their actions. Subsequently, rather than being in control of their emotions they allow their emotions to be in control of them. Alternatively, people who develop emotional intelligence are those who take control of their emotions, thereby also taking control of their thoughts, words and actions. Such people not only control their actions and reactions, but more often than not they also control the direction of any events they are involved in. Therefore, emotional self-control leads to a greater sense of control over life in general.

In order to truly achieve this level of control a person must first learn to establish accountability. Only when you hold yourself accountable for your actions will you truly be in control of them. Any time you deny responsibility for your words or actions you allow those elements to control you, not the other way around. Thus, it is critical that you develop the mindset that embraces accountability rather than one that avoids it. Furthermore, by establishing a sense of self-accountability you can encourage others to become more accountable, thereby spreading the effects of emotional intelligence to all involved.

Always own your mistakes

The first rule of accountability is to always own your mistakes. This is a critical way in which most people lose control of their lives. If you refuse to accept your part in making mistakes you will never learn the lessons that will help you to avoid repeating those mistakes. This means that you will continue to think, speak and act in ways that lead to failure rather than success. Even worse, by running from your mistakes you allow the fear of failure to set in and govern your way of thinking. This is why so many people are gripped with the fear of failure, and why so many seem to repeat their mistakes over and over again.

The most successful people recognize that everyone makes mistakes. As a result, they don't judge others based on the mistakes they make, rather they judge others on how they recover from their mistakes. This is a true sign of emotional as well as intellectual strength. When you own up to your mistakes you first show the courage that many others lack. Subsequently, even though the situation isn't ideal, your attitude will be seen as positive and strong. In the end, this will go a long way to establishing your reputation in the workplace as someone who is courageous, trustworthy and capable of overcoming setbacks. Needless to say, such a reputation will help you to achieve every possible level of success no matter where you work.

Another way that owning your mistakes increases emotional intelligence is that it avoids placing blame on others. All too often you will encounter people who are quick to point the finger when things begin to go wrong. When things are going right, they will be the first to sign their name on the dotted line. However, when mistakes are made or setbacks occur, that's when they let others take center stage. Needless to say, this only destroys a person's reputation as it places them in the category of those who will throw you under the proverbial bus. Such people are never trusted and always treated with disdain. Thus, when you establish accountability you ultimately establish trust.

Embrace imperfection

When you own your mistakes, you establish accountability after the fact, meaning that you claim responsibility after events have taken a turn for the worse. There is a way to establish accountability before the fact, however, which ensures that you own the situation from start to finish. This method is embracing imperfection. When you embrace imperfection, you predict the likelihood that mistakes will be made and setbacks will be encountered. Subsequently, you take responsibility for all possible outcomes even before they occur. This is the true essence of being in total control of any situation you are in.

One of the most important effects of embracing imperfection is that it eliminates the fear of failure. Failure is only seen as a bad thing when you are trying to avoid it at all costs. If, however, you see mistakes and setbacks as a natural part of any endeavor you will eliminate the fear they can create. Furthermore, in addition to eliminating fear such an approach will serve to open your mind to the lessons that can be learned when things go wrong. The simple truth is that you might have to discover what doesn't work before you can discover what does. This can only be accomplished when you are willing to embrace the imperfection of any plan, effort or goal.

Embracing imperfection can be a sure way to create emotional intelligence within others as well. When you assure other people that mistakes are a part of the process, they will become less self-conscious of making them, thereby removing the fear and shame mistakes can cause. Furthermore, by removing the fear and guilt of making mistakes, you will encourage a greater sense of honesty within others. When people aren't afraid to own up to their mistakes, they will be less likely to try to hide them. Instead, they will be eager to find a solution so that they can correct the mistakes and move on. This is the only way that success can ever be truly achieved in the workplace. When people are busy trying to blame others for mistakes or hide their own mistakes, things will only go from bad to worse. However, when everyone is open and honest about every aspect of a project then they can achieve success each and every time. It's simply a matter of owning the situation rather than allowing the situation to own you.

7 IMPROVE OVERALL HEALTH AND WELLBEING

One of the most important lessons regarding emotional intelligence is the simple fact that a person's emotional health and wellbeing is directly connected to their physical health and wellbeing. This is where so many people make their biggest and most devastating mistakes. When a project's deadline is getting dangerously close, and the project still needs far more work before being ready, countless people will work through lunch, work past their schedule, and even skip sleep in order to not be late. While this seems good on paper the fact of the matter is that this is where things can go very wrong very quickly.

Although skipping a meal or some sleep might seem to be a good way to gain time for a project the only thing such steps will accomplish is to make a person more tired, more hungry and subsequently, more stressed. Needless to say, the more stressed a person becomes, the more likely their emotional state will take control of their thoughts, words and actions in a very negative way. Thus, while cutting corners may seem the best option for avoiding failure it can actually prove to be the very cause of failure in the end. Therefore, in order to maintain strong emotional intelligence, you should always avoid cutting corners and instead strive to constantly improve your overall health and wellbeing.

Create a healthy schedule

The first step toward improving overall health and wellbeing is to create a healthy schedule. Numerous studies have shown that when a person works beyond a certain number of hours, both per day and per week, their productivity decreases significantly. Furthermore, the chances of making mistakes will increase after a certain point, meaning that a person's performance will suffer both in terms of quantity and quality. The simple answer to this problem is to make sure that you avoid overworking yourself, no matter the situation.

Ideally you should never work more than eight hours a day, and never work more than five days a week. Additionally, you should take a break every hour and a half in order to stay fresh and alert all throughout the day. And, while having the weekend off may seem like a good thing, the truth is that it is better that you do not work more than three days in a row. This will keep you from getting burned out and becoming sluggish before your workweek comes to an end.

Another critical element of any healthy schedule is to make sure that you get plenty of sleep. Again, most people make the mistake of staying up late to get things finished or waking up extra early in order to catch up on their workload. While this seems reasonable, all it actually does is making the individual more and more sleep deprived. In the end, studies have shown that you will get better results by getting a good night sleep and addressing any issues with full clarity and energy the next day. People who get the right sleep day after day have been shown to produce better results in both quantity and quality. Additionally, their stress levels are always lower, meaning that they are healthier all around.

Finally, there is the all-important element of downtime. Each and every day produces a certain amount of stress on a person no matter how emotionally intelligent they are. The trick is to release that stress through healthy means. As mentioned earlier, laughter is a great way to eliminate stress and fear. Therefore, at some point during the day you should engage in something that allows you to laugh and escape the stresses of your job. Alternatively, reading, playing games or any other number of leisure activities can help you to relax mentally and physically, thereby restoring your energies so that you will be at your best the next day. Thus, you should set aside ample time for such downtime activities each and every day.

Encourage healthy habits

In addition to creating a healthy schedule you need to encourage healthy habits in your daily routine. This will ensure that your energies are healthy and strong, which will help to reduce and even prevent stress and anxiety in your life. One of the best healthy habits that you can practice is eating right. The bottom line is that the food you eat determines your energy levels, how clear your mind is and your ability to resist stress on a daily basis. When your eating habits are unhealthy your body will be sluggish, your mind will be more prone to confusion and you will be more susceptible to negative emotions. Therefore, it is critical to ensure that you eat in a way that is healthy for both your body and mind.

The first step to achieving this goal is to make sure you eat at the right times. Never skip a meal, no matter what the reason might be. Whenever you skip eating you deprive your body and mind of the vital energy they need to function properly. This is no different than skipping sleep. Therefore, always give yourself the time you need to eat breakfast, lunch and dinner.

The next step is to ensure that you eat the right foods. Eating things that contain lots of sugars, fats and chemicals will do more harm than good. Even though your stomach may feel full you won't be providing your mind and body with the energy they need to perform at peak levels. Therefore, be sure to eat foods that are rich in protein, vitamins, minerals and fiber. These elements will provide the physical and mental energy you need to establish strong emotional intelligence. In the end, when you take good care of your body and mind, your emotional wellbeing will improve automatically.

CONCLUSION

Now that you have read this book you have all the tools you need to develop your emotional intelligence. By becoming aware of your emotions and the effects they have on your body and mind you can regain control of your thoughts, words and actions. Additionally, by developing an awareness of the emotional state of others you can greatly improve your interaction with the people in your life, including family, friends and those you work with. Needless to say, emotional intelligence is useful in every area of life, however, the tools provided in this book are especially relevant to the workplace. Therefore, you can now begin to improve your workplace environment whether you are a supervisor, coworker or a regular employee. Furthermore, you can use your emotional intelligence to achieve greater success at work, which will bring greater rewards to your life as a whole. The very best of luck to you and your quest to achieve emotional intelligence!

ZACH ROGER

Emotional Intelligence 2.0

How to Get Rid of Negative Thoughts

Zach Roger

ZACH ROGER

INTRODUCTION

Sometimes, we can be our own worst enemy.

Why have a nemesis who talks behind your back when you can do all the back-talking yourself, right?

And that's the problem with negative thinking. Many of us struggle with a toxic internal monologue that holds us back. We prevent ourselves from moving forward in life by repeating the same tired, self-flagellating negative statements to ourselves. And when we do this, we poison ourselves.

Emotional intelligence is a desirable trait, which allows us to gauge what's going on with those around us and to monitor our own internal landscape. That includes our internal monologue.

To be straight up with you, there's no point in modeling excellent emotional intelligence to those around us if we leave ourselves out of the fun.

So, this book is about a facet of emotional intelligence, which needs to be more thoroughly discussed – how to rid yourself of negative thoughts.

We're going to talk about the ground of emotional intelligence as your ability to regulate your emotions by being alive to them. But we're going a little further than that. We're going to teach you about how to motivate yourself despite your self-doubt and fear of moving forward (generated by that toxic internal monologue).

These are skills you can learn and, in doing so, you'll multiply the valuable quality of emotional intelligence that's so necessary for your success in life. As I've hinted above, approaching yourself with the same tools that you use to gauge other people's emotional status and to apply that information to situations at work and at home is the very root of developing EI to its highest potential. You need to start with yourself to successfully develop your emotional intelligence.

I thank your purchasing, downloading and reading this book. It's my hope that its contents will change the way you look at yourself, so you can change the way you interact with others and move forward in life successfully.

1 YOUR PERSONAL LITANY OF ILLS

A litany is a prayerful recitation. In its traditional, ecclesiastical form, the names of the saints are chanted, as their intercession is requested by the church congregation. But when it comes to negative thoughts, we all have a personal litany of ills.

This litany is very different. While the Litany of the Church asks the saints to deliver us from all manner of evil, the personal litany of ills goes something like this:

Because I'm so inadequate, I may as well not apply for that job.

I really suck at doing that.

Nobody likes me. Everybody hates me. I'm going to eat some worms.

I'm not attractive enough.

I'm not smart enough.

I'm a fraud.

Everyone knows I'm a fraud. They're just too nice to say so.

These are just a few examples of the personal litany of ills, which has become your toxic internal monologue over time. Where do these thoughts come from?

While negative thoughts are self-generated, they have their origins outside of us. The things people say (especially our parents). Personal failures (which are usually minor but which have stuck with us). Negative experiences with other people. Our personal litany of ills can grow rapidly to become a corrosive canon of beliefs we hold about ourselves which are not true.

Or, perhaps, there's a small grain of truth of which we've created a palace of negativity.

Either way, these thoughts hold us back, preventing us from reaching our full potential and being the light in the world we're all capable of being.

Understanding the litany

You weren't born with negative thoughts about yourself. They came from somewhere in your environment.

Parents, teachers, friends, acquaintances, even strangers can set us on a path of negative thinking. While we may not remember the words that triggered the negative thought, our subconscious mind remembers the import of those words.

Thinking of your mind as a palace in which the great room is your conscious mind and the crypt is your subconscious mind is helpful. While the subconscious is deep within your mind's palace, it's often a powerful driver of negative thinking. At any moment, it can assert itself. All it takes is a stray word, or an unexpected interaction and the import of the words, which gave birth to a negative thought resurfaces. You're "triggered" and a flood of negative thinking overwhelms your mind.

The great hall (conscious thinking) is where your ability to reason and to thinking logically reside. This is also where the controls are to your body and its actions. Negative thoughts also hang out in the great room of your mind.

In the crypt (subconscious mind), the controls for involuntary actions like breathing and other systems of the body you rarely think about reside. This is where the "riding a bike" responses live. Once you learn to ride a bicycle, you never forget. It becomes second nature and you what to do to propel the bike and remain upright doesn't even cross your mind. You just get on and ride.

But it's in the crypt that the secret life of your mind lurks, waiting to undermine you with incidents in your life, which have led to your personal litany of ills.

Getting a handle on your mind's secret life is the key to eliminating negative thinking.

Knowing the difference

The first step toward freeing yourself from the toxic influence of negative thinking is the ability to discern the difference between thoughts, which are constructive and build you up and thoughts, which are destructive and tear you down.

At the root of negative thinking are old assertions others have made about you and experiences, which have served to personally indict you (with your full complicity). When these arise as negative thoughts, it's crucial that you understand that what's driving your conscious mind into the crypt is fear.

And there is nothing more negative and threatening than fear.

What you need to know is how that fear is being produced by thoughts and experiences from your past. That means delving into the crypt of your palace for the source of the negative thinking that's doing nothing more valuable than derailing your life's potential.

Cleaning out the crypt

When a negative thought begins to form in your mind, it's accompanied by an emotion. One of those is fear. Another is sadness. But a negative thought is always accompanied by a negative emotion. This toxic feedback loop of negative thinking not only holds you back in life. It can affect your health when it becomes a habit.

So, when these thoughts arise, it's important that you identify, label and above all, challenge them.

This is the work of your conscious mind. Being alive to the negative thought you're having allows you to grab hold of it, examine and challenge it and eliminate it. That's what cleaning out the crypt is all about. It's a long-term project of profound self-examination and improvement.

In our next chapter, we'll be talking about practical ways to clean out your crypt, using tools to help you along the way. Let's get ready to clear out the cobwebs in your crypt and by so doing, stop your personal litany of ills in its tracks, so you can get on with your life.

2 CONFRONTING YOUR MALICIOUS SUBCONSCIOUS

Your attitude toward yourself as a person impacts everything around you. If you believe yourself to be unworthy and incompetent, others pick up on that. You exude the negativity of your beliefs and self-image. So, believing that the world and everyone in it is against you is a bit of a self-fulfilling prophecy. You allow that thought to control you and others notice.

Your beliefs about yourself are rooted in the subconscious mind lurking in the palace crypt.

What you choose to absorb as "real" in terms of the way you think about yourself and your value as a human being is your reality. When you allow your negative thoughts to take the wheel, you are turning those thoughts into immutable beliefs, which are hurting and hindering you.

These beliefs can seem very real. They can seem as though they've been proven beyond the shadow of a reasonable doubt. But the truth is that your personal litany of ills is not real at all. That litany is based on events, which have long passed, other people's invalid and insensitive opinions and statements and your tacit acceptance of them.

I know that because I've had to confront my malicious subconscious in order to tame it and to live the positive reality that is my life. We'll discuss my personal journey a little later. For now, though, let's get down to clearing out the cobwebs in your crypt.

So what?

Negative thoughts almost always cycle through your head as the result of being triggered by incidents and words, which somehow mimic that origin story of those thoughts.

For example, if a teacher in grade school once said you were lazy, similar assertions in your present life can bring that statement back up, galvanizing and validating it.

Your response to the negative thought is: "So what?"

So what if that teacher said that about you? You know it's not true and you have numerous reasons to know that's the case. You know you're not lazy because you throw yourself into what you do for a living, your family and your passions. What's important here is to create a means for reminding yourself that you're not lazy when the negative thought and the corresponding words/incident are triggered.

When the thought arises, just say it. Just say, "So what?" Say it loud. Say it proud.

Then tell yourself why you know you're not lazy and why that teacher was being abusive and unnecessarily cruel. Put the blame for the negative thought on the shoulders of its long-ago progenitor, and leave it there.

Changing the negative thought is work, but it is well worth doing. Your conscious mind needs to override the contents of your subconscious mind to overcome the thought and thus, the self-hating belief.

What you're doing is rejecting the negative thought, which has led to a belief becoming rooted in you. It's in that rejection that you become the master of your own mind, instead of being its unwitting, self-loathing puppet.

The "So what?" may look like a question but what it is, in truth, is an affirmation and validation of the truth you know about yourself. Replacing that negative thought with the knowledge (a conscious act) that you are not that at all is how you move forward and shed negativity as a way of life.

Then again...

At this point, we should remember that sometimes we allow a negative thought to hold us back from changing something about ourselves we don't like.

For example, the belief that you're lazy can become a truth about you. You can absorb that long-ago statement to the degree that you actualize it. If that's the case, the negative thought can be transformative.

The belief that you're lazy may have become a self-fulfilling prophecy and you may have embraced it as an easy way out. That's how you undermine your own efforts and your own life.

Transforming that negative belief calls for some introspection. Looking inside yourself and asking whether you haven't made that false belief settled law (in which you decide it's how you're going to live because you can't do anything about it – because you're too lazy) could change the way you deal with the belief and its destructive presence in your life.

A bit like turning lemons into lemonade, transforming negative thinking into a self-directed project to improve the way you live thoroughly conquers the negativity by turning it into the truth – a positive belief about yourself.

Being honest by recognizing the fact that you've accepted the belief as an excuse to underachieve and live a less-than-fulfilling life is your ticket to freedom. You wrestle the thought to the ground and hit it over the head with a rock. Then, you actively work to change what the belief has wrought in your character.

A clear message

To successfully kill negative beliefs about yourself, it's essential that you be clear in the message you're sending your subconscious. There are no half measures here. There's only a full-throated rejection of the negative belief that's eroding your confidence and self-esteem.

This is where an intentional frame of mind enters the picture. If you're going to clean out the cobwebs in your palace's crypt, you want them all gone. All of them and the nasty spiders who made them. You want that place to be immaculate and re-engineered to support your growing self-confidence.

If you're taking on the fact that you have so internalized the belief that you're lazy, then you can't tell yourself, "I need to stop believing this about myself, but maybe it's too late. Maybe I'm just too lazy to change!"

How useless an approach is that?

To clarify your message, meet any rupture in your resolve with the opposite of your negative thought, as follows:

I am lazy.

I am not lazy. I'm hardworking.

Or, if you've succumbed to the belief and have given it dominion over your life:

I am lazy.

I will transform that laziness into positive action. I will move towards my goals.

It's only when those conscious and unconscious thoughts match - when you've replaced negativity with positivity - that you'll see profound change.

At our cores

At our cores is a set of beliefs about ourselves, which guide us through life.

The negative thinker has unwholesome, negative beliefs about his or her character and worth as a human being. These are formed early on life and derive from the comments and behavior of other people. Our part of the equation is acceptance. And when we're young, we don't have the ability to reason ourselves out of that acceptance and so, we internalize these comments and behaviors as the truth about who we are. We're also very vulnerable to the opinions and attitudes of other people because we so desperately want to be liked and accepted. In that vulnerability is the genesis of negative thinking.

To be able to function as a fully-realized human being, our core beliefs must be positive. Why should anyone else believe in us if we don't believe in ourselves?

Self-affirmations like:

I'm a good person.

People like me.

I work hard.

My work is good.

I'm honest.

These are positive self-beliefs that others can sense in us. If we don't think of ourselves in constructive ways, other people can tell (almost instinctively) that our orientation is negative. That's not attractive. It doesn't inspire confidence or respect.

And it's when we're at our most emotionally vulnerable that the negative beliefs we have about ourselves come to the fore, drowning out the positive. When we're upset, angry or have suffered a personal loss of some kind, a little crack forms in our internal defenses and those negative thoughts and beliefs take over.

The core beliefs we hold true, having been formed prior to becoming adults, are not written in stone. They're written on the delicate psyches of children, well before the age of reason. Having achieved the age of reason, adults are equipped to take an inventory of their negative beliefs about themselves and track their origins.

In doing so, it becomes increasingly clear that some of our most compelling self-perceptions were planted there with errant words. These were not things we thought about ourselves. These were things others said about us.

Along the way, those childhood incidents take root and became our realities. But taking inventory by unpacking your most negative thoughts and systematically rejecting them, recognizes them as unhealthy and unworthy of your attention.

Remember that any belief you have about yourself has no value to you if it doesn't build you up as a person. So, getting to the heart of the matter (where the belief/thought came from) helps you understand that external factors led you to the thought/belief, skewing your self-perception.

And external input, which is thoughtless, careless and false, has no place in your subconscious. It's flotsam. It's ambient junk. It's covered in cobwebs, which must be cleared away.

And the quickest way to do that is to create an inventory of your recurring negative thoughts, identify the source and create a corresponding affirmation.

I'm not going to lie. This is a serious introspective project. By doing it, you'll get to know the truth about yourself. You'll come to know whether the negative thought has become embedded to the point it's a self-fulfilling prophecy. By drilling down into your subconscious crypt with your adult ability to reason and extrapolate information, which is empirical and sound, you can either eliminate or transform the negative thought/belief.

In the next chapter, I'd like to tell you about my own experience of overcoming negative thinking and how it's changed my life immeasurably. I want you to know that you're not alone; that we all struggle with the reality of negative thinking and how powerful an influence it can be in our lives. In that reality is liberation and solidarity, so let me share with you a little of my own experience.

3 HOW I DID IT

Those of us who've struggled with negative thinking have similar stories. One minute we were innocent children, exploring the world with endless energy, curiosity and delight. The next, we were neurotic basket cases, believing with every fiber of our beings that we weren't quite good enough.

So, what happened? I don't know what happened to any of you, but maybe some of what happened to me will sound familiar. It's often the case that hearing one isn't alone is good news, so I'm sharing a bit about my own negative thinking and how eliminating it from my life grew my emotional intelligence by growing my own self-awareness and self-love. The positive frame of mind I wake up with every day is what made that happen, but it demanded a personal journey of introspection and learning how to still the negativity once and for all.

That "ouch" moment

You know as well as I do that there's probably a specific "ouch" moment you go back to for your negative reinforcement. This was a seminal moment in your career as a negative thinker. It was the moment in which your very value as a human being was called into question, propelling you into an adulthood of self-doubt and fear of failure.

For me, that "ouch" moment has lost its sting, but for years, it would be the siren song that routinely turned my mind away from the achievements I should have boldly pursued and toward my personal perceived inadequacies.

I was in elementary school at the time in maybe Grade 4. I was smart and over-achieving. As precocious and exploratory as they come, I knew I was headed for the big time. I didn't know what that might be, but I was already thinking of careers like law. My world had no ceiling.

And then, I was confronted by a teacher who wanted to "help" me by detaining me every day after school to work on my lisp.

My lisp, at the time, was pronounced and slightly embarrassing but the other kids didn't tease me about it much. It was just part of who I was. But this teacher decided that I could not have a lisp; that I needed to learn how to "properly" pronounce "s" sounds. But the longer this went on, the more frustrated I became. I couldn't make that sound like most people and frankly, I hadn't even thought too much about it until that first day when this teacher so helpfully brought to my attention that I was "doing it wrong."

Finally, I refused to attend these sessions any longer, with the full support of my parents. Of course, I had to go home at the point of tears for that to happen.

While his intentions may have been noble, the damage done by the episode stuck with me for years. I loved singing but was afraid to try. I loved being in the drama club but feared opening my mouth in front of an audience. I struggled to answer questions in class, looking for ways to avoid the letter "s" at all costs. I would carefully construct my sentences to avoid it as much as humanly possible.

There were many other "ouchy" moments in my life, to be sure, but the "lisp episode" was by far the most impactful. It was to wound me for many years, as I struggled to be who I knew I could be, afraid to open my mouth the whole time.

And that won't get you far in life.

Recognizing the wound

It wasn't until I was on the cusp of my 30s that a friend mentioned a trait he'd noticed in me. He said, "You always choose the storm cloud over the silver lining."

I was a little taken aback, but when I asked him what he meant, he explained that while I usually seemed happy and positive, he knew that wasn't the case. Whenever an opportunity to change my life would come up, I'd make excuses. I'd weave a tale of worst-case scenarios, which would probably arise the moment I reached out for the opportunity.

I thought about it. I thought about what my friend had said to me, reeling it out in my mind and checking it for holes. But I knew he was right and the more I thought about it, the more I thought about the "lisp episode." The more I realized that this was the wound in myself I needed to reconcile in order to move forward.

Was I still laboring under a misguided teacher's attempt to fix me? Was I still treating that episode as though I needed to be fixed? Was I still in 4th Grade?

I supposed I was. I supposed that my potential had been voluntarily frozen in time. I say voluntarily because I was moving into my 30s. My 4th Grade self couldn't have been expected to have the psychological muscle to wrestle that "ouch" moment to the ground. But surely, my adult self was up to it?

I decided that, yes. I was up to it. And that's when my life began to change.

Self-compassion

We tend to think of compassion as a human effort that flows outward. "Feeling with" other people is a noble quality and one which makes the world a better place to live.

But how can you model compassion for others when you have none for yourself?

Self-compassion is about healing the wound your "ouch" moment created. As I've said, we've all had more than one "ouch" moment, but they tend to throw the original wound into relief, making it more menacingly 3-dimensional. It's that original wound which seeks the validation of more negativity. It attracts it like a magnet.

The wounded, negative thinker seeks more negativity in order to validate the beliefs they've accumulated about themselves. Instead of rejecting the original wound, they pile on the scar tissue every time a stray word or action comes their way.

Every romantic involvement that fails. Every friendship that ends. Every employment rejection, firing and incident of professional discipline. Every jerk that cuts you off in traffic. Every coffee order the barista gets wrong.

It all adds up to one big, negative ball of angst that you do your best to keep at bay by putting on a happy face, all the while believing yourself to be inadequate and unworthy.

But what I learned on my journey away from negative thinking is that self-compassion is the balm your wound needs to heal.

Who am I?

Your starting point in the project of putting a lid on the negative thinking and beliefs which are derailing your life is to answer the question, "Who am I?"

Creating an inventory of positive personal achievements and attributes is a powerful weapon against the self-destructive tendency to view yourself in a negative light. You will need a pad of paper and a pen or pencil.

Think about all the things you've done in your life that you're proud of.

These can be anything from turning up for work on time, all the time, to passing your driver's test. Allow your mind to go to the moments that lifted you up and made you feel you were worthwhile, after all.

Now, write down your most positive traits. Are you neat? Write it down. Are you a good worker? Are you reliable? Are you honest? All these things are positive traits and they count because what you write about yourself is your truth, when you focus on what you like about who you are.

Here's the thing – my 4th Grade self didn't care about my lisp until someone told that poor kid that it was unacceptable by trying to fix it. I can give that teacher the benefit of the doubt or I can think he had some weird problem with people who lisp. In the end, it doesn't matter. What matters is my own conception of what it means to have a lisp. And giving that teacher the benefit of the doubt is the right thing to do because it heals the resentment.

It neutralizes the wound's source as being just as fragile, human and fallible as I am.

I still lisp. I don't care, though. I accept the way I speak and most others do, too. The occasional person who points it out tends to be a socially inept clod, which is their problem – not mine. I've never attended speech therapy, either because I now think of my lisp as just another fabulous, funky part of who I am.

And that was possible because I healed the wound with self-compassion. To do that, I didn't just need to sit down that one time to write out positive things about myself. I had to actively remind myself, every day, that I was exactly where I was supposed to be in that moment because I was worthy.

And where I was excited me. I was on the edge of finding out just how far I could go because I'd finally healed that "ouch" moment. So, I continued with my positive affirmations about who I genuinely am, every day. I started a journal.

And it's your journal that's going to be your best friend, as you move toward giving yourself the same compassion you usually reserve for other people.

A daily project

I tend to think of journaling as an activity for the evenings when the day is almost done and you're just about ready to turn in. I sit in a comfortable place, empty my mind of extraneous thoughts and simply jot down the high points of my day.

Once I'm through the high points, I note the low points. They usually pale in comparison to the truly great moments.

After I've gone through the chronological review of my day, I identify moments in which my positive attributes and abilities were in play and how they made the day even better.

In short, I blow my own horn.

And if your "ouch" moment is someone telling you not to be so crazy about yourself, then knowing fully that you have good reason to be is the antidote.

I'm not telling you to be a narcissist (those people aren't at all well). I'm telling you to appreciate and love yourself as the worthy person you are. You have something in you that the world needs. If you're a negative thinker (as I once was), then you need to leave that "ouch" moment and all the scar tissue that original wound has accumulated behind. You need to replace it with the knowledge of what your value and contribution can become.

Reviewing your day every evening keeps you honest and away from the negative thinking that's been holding you back. Making note of how your aptitudes and talents changed the course of the day or made it better (in even the smallest way) is a self-esteem builder that helps you re-tool your frame of mind. Killing negativity with a positive way of seeing yourself and what you bring to the party is an effective support, when done each day, intentionally.

And intention is extremely important in this model. You need to mean it. You need to believe it and you need to do it. You need to know in your heart that you want to excuse the negativity from your mind and your life.

So, blow your own horn as I did and continue to do. Believe in yourself and stop believing the old stories, which have roosted in your head because of something that happened too long ago to care about. You are free to be who you truly are, unimpeded by the thoughtless intervention or negative aspersions of others.

Next, let's explore how turning off negative thinking makes room for emotional intelligence that's been informed by your own journey.

4 ALERT AND ATTENTIVE

"Ask yourself, is there negativity in me at this moment? Then, become alert and attentive to your thoughts as well as your emotions."
Eckhart Tolle

Eckhart Tolle's simple prescription in the quote shown above is all about self-regulation. Without self-regulation, your emotions rule you. You lose control and you also lose the social capital you need to succeed.

Your thoughts and emotions work closely together, creating the framework for the moment you're living in, right now. When your thoughts are negative, it's likely that your emotions will follow suit and that toxic feedback will never close unless you do the important work of self-regulation.

This isn't a "pie in the sky" type of discussion, folks. The idea that you're able to self-regulate your thoughts and emotions is a scientifically proven reality. In truth, if you can self-regulate, you can "re-wire" your neural pathways to permanently gain control of the quality of your thinking and of the attending emotions.

Executive control training

Published in the journal NeuroImage, a January 2016 study conducted at the Ben-Gurion University of the Negev in Israel monitored the brain activity of a group of 26 volunteers.

The study used executive control training to affect the way study participants responded to negative stimuli. Executive control training correlates to the Buddhist practice of mindfulness, which allows the brain to detach from negative or unpleasant stimuli. This sense of detachment amounts to intellectual and emotional regulation.

Some participants in the Ben-Gurion study followed a more intense type of training. During the study, the amygdala (associated with negative emotions like anxiety and sadness) showed drastically reduced activity when confronted by the study's examples of negativity. In addition, the amygdala was seen to be more effectively connected to the part of the frontal cortex implicated in emotional regulation.

The study's findings have numerous real-world applications, including the treatment of clinically depressed people and those struggling with PTSD (Post-Traumatic Stress Disorder).

But what's genuinely astounding about this study and its findings is that it undergirds the idea that the brain is plastic organ (subject to change). The structures and connections of the brain and how they work can be reinvented by training people to self-regulate and to choose not to attach to negative thoughts and the emotions that come with them.

In other words, you can re-train your brain to think positively and optimistically instead of negatively and pessimistically. This re-training needn't even be formal. My own efforts prove that and soon, yours will too.

Think first

Negative thinkers tend to pre-judge every situation as being inherently threatening or unfavorable. They further allow their thinking to adhere to their emotions, which they then reveal inappropriately and sometimes, self-destructively.

Acting on impulse is a tremendous problem for many people. This begins in childhood and unless a child is actively taught self-regulation and mindfulness about how others perceive impulsive behavior, it can endure into adulthood.

But as adults, shouldn't we be held accountable for our conduct? Shouldn't we be able to stop, think and prevent emotional outbursts, which not only cast us in a bad light but harm those around us?

Of course, we should. Some of us just need to work a little harder at it than others.

Adults who lose their cool under pressure aren't going to be considered for the top-flight positions, which demand the ability to, self-regulate. In fact, self-regulation is one of the most important components of emotional intelligence. Starting with our self-awareness and ability to detect and halt the formation of negative thoughts and emotions, we enhance our ability to detect the emotional states of others. Self-awareness and self-regulation lead to a heightened awareness of where those around us are, emotionally and help us to address the meaning and potential consequences of their emotions.

Mind yourself

Mindfulness is the ability to live in the moment as it is. Without embellishment, mindfulness allows us to see the truth in every moment we live and in so doing, the truth others are living concurrently.

Mindfulness can be encouraged with tools like deep breathing, journaling (as we've discussed) and taking a moment to think before responding to any given statement or situation. All these tools force our brains to relax, instead of seeking the instant gratification being demanded by our negative thinking and emotions. At the core of mindfulness is being alert to your internal monologue and actively seeking to regulate and reform it.

Reappraising

Pragmatism is the ability to process information that competes with your appraisal of any given situation and absorb it. By stepping back from your personal viewpoint and taking a 360-degree tour of factors you may not have taken note of, you're better equipped to navigate it appropriately, without negativity knocking it all sideways.

A big part of the ability to reappraise situations and scenarios is to give others the benefit of the doubt. For example, it's possible that the co-worker you believe disrespected you by not acknowledging your contribution to a project didn't know what your contribution was. That guy on the bus who banged into you may have a balance issue that caused the collision. Your dry cleaning isn't ready because there was a technical issue.

In other words, it's not all about you. The world is not out to get you. There are factors involved which make the situation, scenario or incident innocuous and these factors are what transform the complexion of what you've misinterpreted as a personal comment on you.

No, Virginia. It's really not all about you!

Instead of having a confrontation, or building up resentment against others, a reappraisal allows you to step back and see things as they really are before allowing yourself to spiral into a negative frenzy of self-loathing and recriminations against yourself and others.

How does self-regulation change you?

Being able to effectively self-regulate changes everything. Once you've become more skilled at it, you'll stop thinking everyone's against you or dislikes you and start seeing them as the benign entities they are.

You'll see the challenges that come up in life, work and love as opportunities to grow. You'll be a better communicator who doesn't sit on resentments but gets to the heart of the matter by talking about whatever's happened to the person or people it happened with.

When you're able to mindfully regulate your toxic internal monologue and reform it to become something positive and optimistic, you'll find that you're clear about your goals and will act according to your self-professed values and morals.

And even if you don't believe it will benefit you in any significant way, you do your best. You don't do a half-assed job because you must. You do a great job because you want to and because you can.

Best of all you, your mindfulness will lead to greater contentment and satisfaction. When you stop your toxic internal monologue, you start the nurturing internal monologue, which leads to inner calm and the ability to overcome the bad times (because you know that good times are right behind them).

The element of choice

Everything in this book is leading to one conclusion – that you have a choice. You have a choice to think the negative thoughts you allow to rule you. And you have a choice to allow your negative emotions to rule you. Choosing a better way forward is why you're here.

You and you alone are responsible for your own words, reactions and thoughts. While you may feel that life has been tough on you and that you're at a disadvantage, that's your choice too. You can choose to reject this kind of self-undermining mindset, exchanging it for one, which will propel you forward.

When you feel the negativity in you rising, know that you define the outcome. You say whether that negativity gets to come out to play. Self-awareness and alertness to the thoughts that crowd your head at difficult moments leads to understanding that these moments are minor players in the great sweep of your life story. But those same difficult moments can be self-fulfilling prophets of doom when you fail to regulate yourself and let the dark cloud over your head win the day.

In choosing to be the master of your thoughts and emotions, you're choosing to live a more fruitful life. Negative thinking and the emotions that come with it may have become your daily reality. Maybe you think you're stuck with it.

But that's a choice too. And it's a negative choice.

You have within you the ability to overcome negative thinking to move into a brighter future. Change is not easy. No one ever said it was. But I know it's possible because I've lived it. I've learned to detect moments, which have the potential to resurrect my inner demons. Detaching from them, hearing what's really being said and seeing things as they are (and not as I'd formerly conditioned myself to believe they were) is the royal road to using my limited energy for more fruitful, positive pursuits.

If I can manage it, I know darned well you can, too.

I'm grateful that you've downloaded this book and that you've read this far. I know that you're as able as anyone else to reform your negative thinking patterns in favor of an emotionally intelligent approach to life that builds up instead of tearing down. All you need to do is make the decision to proceed.

And if you've read this far, I know that decision has been made.

CONCLUSION

Negativity thinking is one of the most corrosive habits people can get into. It damages relationships at home and at work. It damages self-esteem and it hinders career progress.

But so many of us engage in it as a way of life. The cobwebbed crypt cries out for recognition and we respond by allowing it to invade the great room of our palace. And you've grown weary of it, which is why you're here. You ardently desire change and I trust that the contents of this book have given you an idea as to how you might go about it.

Having been a victim of my own negative thinking, I'm aware of just how destructive it can be. So, doing something for yourself to change its toxic presence in your life by evicting it from your mind is a positive step forward. It's a step you've already taken just by choosing to read this book.

But you have many more steps to take to get into the valuable habit of self-regulation and the ability to see things are they really are and not as you've become conditioned to seeing them.

There is world out there waiting for what you have to offer. Your gifts and aptitudes are unique and they're desperately needed. But to offer them wholeheartedly, your belief in yourself and your way of seeing the world must change.

Taming your personal litany of ills and your malicious sub-conscious are at the heart of being able to gift yourself with the same compassion you show others. You deserve it, too. You deserve a life, which has been freed of the toxicity of negative thinking. Self-regulating effectively and being pragmatic about what happens out there in the world are important skills that the most sought-after talent is in command of.

And soon, you will be too.

Trust in the future. Believe in yourself. Give others the benefit of the doubt. Know that you're just one more fragile human life on the planet but a life with much to offer a world in need of optimism and positivity. Leaving negativity behind, you're choosing to strike out for the higher ground you know you can get to.

You've got this!

www.ingramcontent.com/pod-product-compliance
Lightning Source LLC
Chambersburg PA
CBHW071255070526
44583CB00017B/2475